NARUTO™

VOL. 4
THE NEXT LEVEL

STORY AND ART BY

SAKURA サクラ

Smart and studious, Sakura is the brightest of Naruto's classmates, but she's constantly distracted by her crush on Sasuke. Her goal: to win Sasuke's heart!

NARUTO ナルト

When Naruto was born, a destructive fox spirit was imprisoned inside his body. Spurned by the older villagers, he's grown into an attention-seeking troublemaker. His goal: to become the village's next *Hokage*.

SASUKE サスケ

The top student in Naruto's class, Sasuke comes from the prestigious Uchiha clan. His goal: to get revenge on a mysterious person who wronged him in the past.

KAKASHI カカシ

The elite ninja assigned to train Naruto, Sasuke, and Sakura. His *sharingan* ("mirror-wheel eye") allows him to reflect and mimic enemy *ninjutsu*.

ZABUZA 再不斬

A ruthless ninja assassin and mass-murderer known as "The Demon." He specializes in techniques involving water and mist.

HAKU 白

A mysterious orphan who befriends Naruto. Naruto doesn't realize that his new friend is Zabuza's loyal masked assistant, who fights with chiropractic needles.

TAZUNA タズナ

An old bridge-builder struggling to bring prosperity to the Land of Waves. The evil millionaire Gato has hired Zabuza to stop him from completing his newest bridge.

THE STORY SO FAR...

Twelve years ago, a destructive nine-tailed fox spirit attacked the ninja village of Konohagakure. The *Hokage*, or village champion, defeated the fox by sealing its soul into the body of a baby boy. Now that boy, Uzumaki Naruto, has grown up to become a ninja-in-training, learning the art of *ninjutsu* with his classmates Sakura and Sasuke.

Tired of easy exercises, Naruto and his classmates make the mistake of asking their teacher, Kakashi, for a really hard assignment... and find themselves in the Land of Waves, protecting a bridge-builder named Tazuna. But the job turns truly dangerous when the notorious assassin Zabuza shows up. While Kakashi holds off Zabuza and Sakura protects Tazuna, Naruto and Sasuke face Zabuza's assistant Haku. In the battle, Sasuke sacrifices himself to save Naruto from Haku's deadly throwing needles. Now, watching his classmate fall, Naruto feels something terrible stir within him...

NARUTO

VOL. 4
THE NEXT LEVEL

CONTENTS

GOONG
28: NINE TAILS...!!
ONG ONG ONG
!
WH...WHAT CHAKRA IS THIS?!
SHFF

Number 28: Nine Tails...!!

READ THIS WAY

!
!!
!!
NO!
NO... THIS POWER - THIS ENERGY... IS... FOUL... IT'S EVIL. AND... FAMILIAR... BUT IT CAN'T BE!
IS THIS... ZABUZA'S DOING?!
...!!

READ THIS WAY
THIS CHAKRA I'M FEELING. SOMETHING ABOUT IT... FILLS ME WITH DREAD!
KAKASHI...?!
NO... IT SEEMS BIGGER THAN KAKASHI, SOMEHOW. BUT WHO --?!
NARUTO!!
UNBELIEVABLE. IT CAN'T BE! AFTER ALL THIS TIME--
- HAS THE BINDING SPELL BEGUN TO UNRAVEL? IS THE SEAL BROKEN?
!
...
...I SENSE...
I SENSE THAT WE'RE SAFE - FOR NOW. IT HASN'T BROKEN THROUGH YET... NOT COMPLETELY.
BUT THE SEAL HAS SLIPPED A LITTLE, OR CRACKED. AND THE POWER OF THE NINE-TAILED DEMON FOX IS BLEEDING THROUGH.

SPLAT
KLAT
SHLUK
FWUP FWP
PLIT
IF I ACT QUICKLY, THERE'S STILL A CHANCE --!
...I'M A BUSY MAN. YOU'RE A BUSY MAN. WE'VE BOTH GOT A LOT ON OUR PLATES...
LISTEN TO ME... ZABUZA...

READ THIS WAY

... AND IT GOES AGAINST THE GRAIN TO EVEN SUGGEST THIS...
...BUT WHAT DO YOU SAY WE STOP SCREWING AROUND...
FWUP FWP FWP FWP
POK
...AND WRAP THIS UP RIGHT NOW? ONE BIG MOVE, WINNER TAKE ALL?
BAM
AN INTRIGUING NOTION...
WHAT'S LEFT, KAKASHI?
SHOW ME WHAT YOU'VE GOT!
GONGONGONG

GRRRR
HE'S ATTACKING!!!
CHUK
TAK

FWOOSH!
HE'S SO BLOODTHIRSTY! HE'S COMPLETELY CHANGED FROM THE BOY OF JUST MINUTES AGO!
RAAAAH
POW!
HE... HE DEFLECTED THEM... WITHOUT EVEN TOUCHING THEM?!
!
GLARE

BOOOOOM
TUMBLE
THUD
SKIIIIID
I'VE GOT TO MAKE IT TO THE NEXT MIRROR!
TAK

SHLUK!!
HE COULDN'T HAVE--!!
GRRRR

AAAUUURGH!!
ONGONGONG
KREAK
POP

I CAN'T WITHSTAND HIS CHAKRA ANY MORE!!!
PLIT PLIT
THIS IS BAD!!!
!
PLIT
UHN...
KRUNCH
OW...
!!
HEH

SKID SKID SKID
KRAK
SHHM
SH

READ THIS WAY

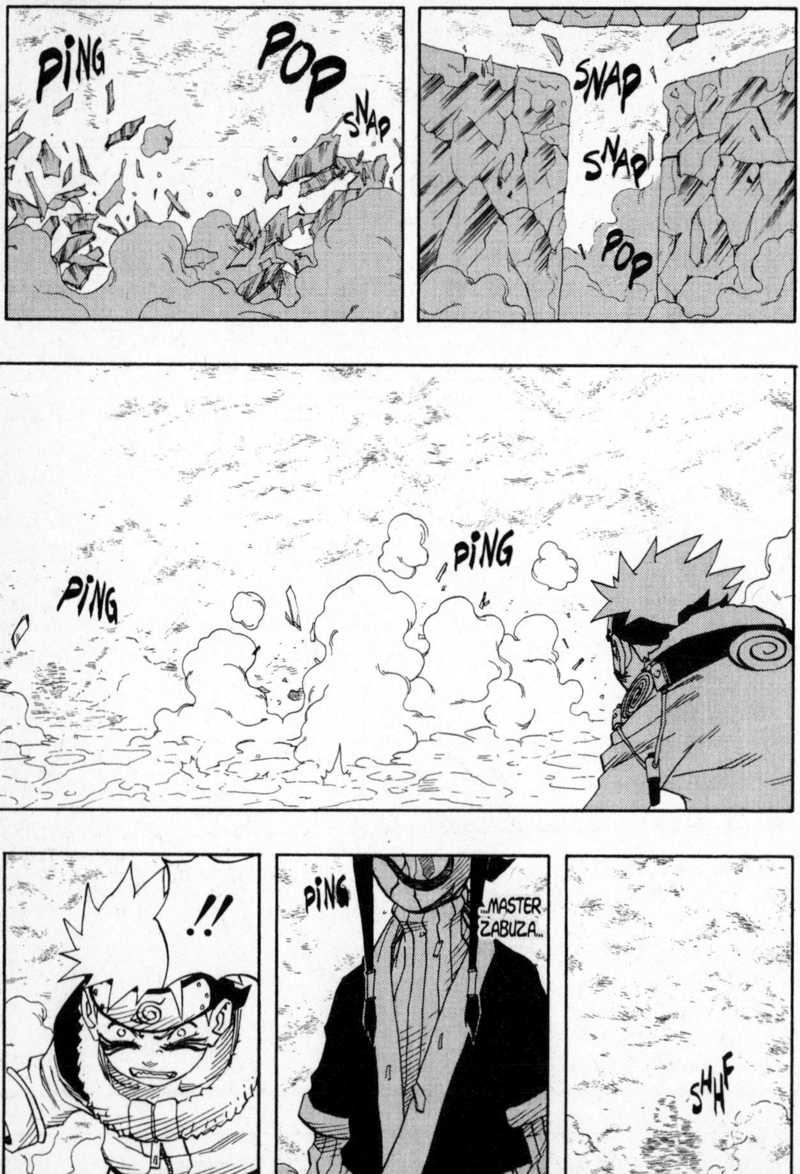

TAK
...I...
...AM FINISHED.

MASTER ZABUZA...
PING

KISHIMOTO MASASHI'S FIRST MANGA REJECT SPECIAL!

THE CHARACTER DESIGNS TO THE LEFT ARE FROM A FAILED PROJECT OF MINE CALLED "WANDERING DETOUR" THAT I CAME UP WITH RIGHT AFTER I WON THE HOP-STEP STAR AWARD.

THE STORY IS ABOUT WHAT HAPPENS WHEN AN ELEMENTARY SCHOOL KID NAMED AKIRA AND HIS FRIENDS KATCHIN AND KAORU FIND A WALLET ON THE WAY HOME FROM SCHOOL, AND OF ALL OF THE TROUBLE THAT ENSUES WHEN THE THREE OF THEM DECIDE TO KEEP THE MONEY THAT THEY FIND AND SPEND IT ON THEMSELVES. MAYBE IT WAS TOO HARD TO FOLLOW, OR SIMPLY TOO DOWN-TO-EARTH FOR A BOYS' ADVENTURE MAGAZINE... BUT FOR WHATEVER REASON, IT WAS SUMMARILY REJECTED.

IT WAS MY FIRST REJECTION EVER. BUT I WAS SUCH A KID BACK THEN, EVEN GETTING MY FIRST REJECTION SEEMED LIKE A BIG DEAL, ANOTHER PROFESSIONAL MILESTONE I'D PASSED. FOR THE LONGEST TIME, I'D BEEN READING OTHER MANGA CARTOONISTS' TALES OF WOE ABOUT THE REJECTIONS THEY'D GOTTEN, AND I'D BEEN FEELING A LITTLE LEFT OUT. WITH "WANDERING DETOUR," I WAS FINALLY IN THE CLUB! I EVEN BRAGGED ABOUT IT A LITTLE. LIKE I SAID, I WAS A KID THEN. NOW, I'M A TRUE PROFESSIONAL, AND I AGREE WITH MY FRIENDS: "REJECTION SUCKS!" (LAUGHTER)

Number 29:
Someone Precious To You

MASTER ZABUZA...
I...
I'M...
PLIT

SHIIIIN
WOOOOM
SKF
SKF

Y-YOU'RE... THE KID I MET THIS MORNING...!!
...
...
WHY DID YOU STOP?

I MURDERED YOUR COMRADE... YOUR BELOVED FRIEND...
... AND YOU STILL SPARE ME?!
SLAM
CRAAAAAP!!
POW
KOFF!!

ALL THE POWER YOU HAD BEFORE... WHERE IS IT? YOU CAN'T HOPE TO KILL ME WITH THE MEAGER FORCE YOU PUT INTO THAT BLOW.
SHF
!
...DO YOU HAVE... ANYONE SPECIAL IN YOUR LIFE?
I'M WILLING TO DO WHATEVER IT TAKES... TO PROTECT THE ONE I CARE ABOUT MOST....
DOING SO IS MY OWN DREAM.
HUFF
OFTEN PEOPLE HAVE IT WRONG, MISTAKENLY BELIEVING...
... THAT SHOWING MERCY TO AN ENEMY IS KINDNESS.
THEY SPARE THE FOE WHOSE LIFE IS IN THEIR HANDS...
BUT DON'T YOU SEE?
IT'S AN EMPTY EXISTENCE...
SHA
...TO GO ON LIVING... ALONE AND UNLOVED... WHEN DEFEAT'S ALREADY COST YOU YOUR DREAM!

HEH
YOU'VE TAKEN AWAY MY REASON FOR LIVING!
MASTER ZABUZA HAS NO USE FOR A WEAK SHINOBI.
SAY WHAT--?!
THAT MERCENARY SCUMBAG DOESN'T CARE WHO HE WORKS FOR OR WHO GETS HURT, JUST SO SOMEONE PAYS HIM!
WHY WASTE ALL THAT DEVOTION ON SUCH A CREEP?!
!!
WHEN PEOPLE ARE PROTECTING SOMETHING TRULY PRECIOUS TO THEM, THEY TRULY CAN BECOME... AS STRONG AS THEY MUST BE!
WHY...
...
IS THAT BROWLESS WONDER REALLY PRECIOUS TO YOU - YOUR "BELOVED FRIEND?!!!"

...
ONCE... I WAS PRECIOUS. I BELONGED... TO...
!
MY...
...
...PARENTS.
!
...
I WAS BORN IN A SNOWY, LITTLE VILLAGE IN THE LAND OF MIST.
AND I WAS HAPPY... MY PARENTS WERE GOOD, KIND PEOPLE.

JUST AS I WAS GETTING OLD ENOUGH TO REALLY NOTICE THE WORLD AROUND ME...
...SOMETHING HAPPENED.
BUT...
...BLOOD...?!
BLOOD. MY BLOOD.
...
WHAT HAPPENED?
...LIKE WHAT...?
WHAT ARE YOU TALKING ABOUT?!
SO...
...

MY FATHER KILLED MY MOTHER...
...AND TRIED TO KILL ME.
WHY--?
THE LAND OF THE MIST HAS BEEN THE SCENE OF GENERATIONS OF NON-STOP WAR. AMONG ITS PEOPLE, THOSE WHO POSSESS THE KEKKEI GENKAI - SKILLS THAT COME OUT OF OUR GENETIC INHERITANCE - ARE LOATHED AS ABOMINATIONS.
"KEKKEI GENKAI"...?!
THE TERM REFERS TO CLANS WHOSE BLOODLINES GIVE THEM POWERS LIKE MINE.
INHERITED SKILLS THAT WERE EXPLOITED AND TWISTED, USED TO CAUSE HORRIBLE SLAUGHTER...
...UNTIL WE CEASED TO BE LOOKED ON AS WARRIORS OR EVEN WEAPONS, BUT WERE CONDEMNED AS THE HARBINGERS OF DOOM.
AFTER THE WARS WERE OVER, WE WHO POSSESSED THIS TRAIT WERE HUNTED, ONLY ABLE TO SURVIVE BY HIDING THE EXISTENCE OF OUR SKILLS AND OUR BLOODLINE AWAY.
EXPOSURE MEANT CERTAIN DEATH!
I'M SURE THE BOY I KILLED, WHO SHARED THAT SKILL, MUST ALSO HAVE GROWN UP KNOWING THE PAIN OF WHICH I SPEAK.
WE ARE SPECIAL. WE ARE POWERFUL. AND WE ARE FEARED.

MY FATHER LEARNED... THAT MY MOTHER...
...CAME FROM SUCH A CLAN... AND BEFORE I EVEN REALIZED WHAT I WAS ABOUT TO DO...
MY FATHER HAD DIED... BY MY HAND.
AND THEN IT CAME TO ME.
I KNEW WHAT I WAS.
...
AND I WAS FORCED TO ACCEPT IT.
THAT WAS THE MOST PAINFUL THING...
THE MOST PAINFUL THING...?
ACCEPTING THAT I WAS ALONE IN THE WORLD.
SUPERFLUOUS. UNWANTED. SHUNNED.

!!
HE... SOUNDS... THE WAY I FEEL!
DIDN'T YOU TELL ME...
THAT YOU WANTED TO BECOME THE NUMBER ONE NINJA IN YOUR VILLAGE AND MAKE EVERYONE RESPECT YOU?
IF YOU HAD SOMEONE IN YOUR LIFE WHO DID MORE THAN THAT... WHO ACKNOWLEDGED YOUR EXISTENCE - EVEN CARED FOR YOU --
-- WOULDN'T THAT PERSON BECOME THE MOST IMPORTANT... TREASURED... PERSON IN YOUR LIFE?!
...MASTER ZABUZA ADOPTED ME, KNOWING I CAME FROM A KEKKEI GENKAI BLOODLINE.
THE VERY THING IN ME THAT MADE EVERYONE ELSE HATE ME - HE DIDN'T JUST OVERLOOK IT. HE CHERISHED IT. HE WANTED IT!

FROM THIS DAY ON, YOU BELONG TO ME, BODY, SOUL... AND BLOOD!
COME!
!!
I WAS SO HAPPY...!!
I HAVE BAD NEWS FOR YOU, HAKU... I'M LEAVING THIS LAND TONIGHT!
BUT...! I'VE SWORN AN OATH TO RETURN ONE DAY... AS A CONQUERER, WHO'LL CRUSH THEM ALL BENEATH MY FEET!
AND TO DO THAT, WHAT I NEED FROM YOU IS NEITHER LOVE NOR AFFECTION AND SUPPORT. WHAT I REQUIRE IS--!
I UNDER-STAND.

I AM YOUR WEAPON AND YOUR TOOL.
KEEP ME BESIDE YOU, AND I'LL STRIKE WHERE YOU TELL ME TO STRIKE, KILL WHOM YOU TELL ME TO KILL.
HEH...
GOOD BOY.
FORGIVE ME... MASTER ZABUZA... YOUR TOOL HAS FAILED YOU.
NARUTO...
PLEASE...
TAKE MY LIFE.
!

SWUP
SWUP
SWUP
SWUP
ONG
SHINOBI CONJURATION!
EARTH STYLE! FANGED VENGEANCE TECHNIQUE!

THIS POSTURING WILL GET YOU NOWHERE, KAKASHI!
YOU CAN'T EVEN TELL WHERE I TRULY AM!!!
WHILE I, ON THE OTHER HAND, KNOW EXACTLY WHERE YOU ARE AND EXACTLY HOW TO DEFEAT YOU!!!
YOU ARE COMPLETELY ENMESHED IN MY SPELL!
!!
ONGONGONG
EH--?!
WHOOM
NO!!!!

WSH
SNAP
SNARF
KRAM
!!!!
GRAB
!
WH-WHAT ARE WE HEARING?
WHEN YOUR EYES AND YOUR EARS HAVE LET YOU DOWN --
-- YOU CAN ALWAYS FOLLOW YOUR NOSE!

UHN...
THIS CONJURATION IS SPECIFICALLY DESIGNED FOR TRACKING.
IT WORKED BECAUSE YOU SHUT YOUR EYES IN THE MIST.

UHN...
THE SMELL OF MY BLOOD IS ALL OVER YOU AND YOUR WEAPONS, SO THICK...
...MY LITTLE NINJA PUPS COULDN'T MISS IT!
IT'S WHY I WENT OUT OF MY WAY TO BLEED A BIT DURING BOTH OF OUR EARLIER ENCOUNTERS.
EVERY DOG HAS HIS NOSE... AND THEY ALL KNOW YOU STINK.
SO... WHO'S ENMESHED IN WHOSE SPELL NOW?
UGH...
THE FOG IS LIFTING. I CAN SEE YOUR FUTURE...
YOUR FUTURE IS DEATH.

KISHIMOTO MASASHI'S SECOND MANGA REJECT SPECIAL.

THE DESIGN TO THE LEFT IS FROM ANOTHER FLOP - A MANGA CALLED "ASIAN PUNK", THAT WAS RESOUNDINGLY REJECTED AT EVERY TURN. TO BE FRANK, THE PREMISE WAS—NOT COINCIDENTALLY—KINDA LIKE "GHOSTBUSTERS."

THE MAIN CHARACTER WAS A KID WITH AN AXE TAKING ON AN EVIL FENG-SHUI MASTER WHO COULD SUMMON AND CONTROL EVIL SPIRITS... AND THE MAIN CHARACTER WASN'T REALLY HUMAN HIMSELF, BUT HAD BEEN CREATED BY SOME GREATER POWER. THERE WAS MORE, BUT WE DON'T NEED TO GO INTO IT HERE.

THE THING IS, WITH THAT STORY, MY PRIZE-WINNING SERIES KARAKUR, AND NARUTO, IT OCCURS ME TO ME THAT MY HEROES ARE ALWAYS THESE YOUNG GUYS. I GUESS I'M JUST A SUCKER FOR BOYS' ADVENTURE TALES!

Number 30: Your Future is...!!

YOU SAY MY FUTURE IS DEATH...?
I'VE HAD ENOUGH OF YOUR BLUFFS.
WHO'S BLUFFING NOW?
THERE'S NO WAY OUT. FACE IT.
YOU'RE GOING TO DIE.
ZABUZA...
YOU'VE HAD YOUR FUN.

...
YOU SCHEMED YOUR SCHEMES...
THE DAY YOU DESERTED THE LAND OF THE MIST AND BECAME A TURNCOAT AND RENEGADE, YOUR NAME AND YOUR ACTIONS WERE REPORTED TO US AT KONOHA VILLAGE.
WE KNOW ALL ABOUT THE FAILED COUP YOU AND YOUR FOLLOWERS STAGED, AND ABOUT THE ATTEMPT TO ASSASSINATE MIZUKAGE, THE WATER SHADOW, LEADER OF YOUR PEOPLE.
YOU'VE BEEN TRYING TO RAISE FUNDS FOR A SECOND ATTEMPT, AND BARELY STAYING A JUMP AHEAD OF THE SHINOBI HUNTERS... WHICH IS WHAT BROUGHT YOU HERE.
IT'S WHY YOU'D STOOP TO WORK FOR A PARASITE LIKE GATÔ.
FWUP
FWUP
FWUP
RRRRRM
RRRRRRM

LIGHTNING BLADE!
YOU'RE A LOOSE CANNON...
SIZZLE.
I CAN ALMOST SEE... THE CHAKRA IN HIS PALM...!
WH-WHAT THE!!
!!
AND THE BRIDGE YOU'RE TRYING TO PREVENT HIM FROM COMPLETING IS THE LAND'S HOPE.
THE MAN YOU'RE TRYING TO KILL, MR. TAZUNA, IS THE HEART AND SPIRIT OF THIS PLACE.

THAT'S NOT WHAT A TRUE SHINOBI DOES.
YOU'RE WILLING TO SACRIFICE THIS PLACE AND EVERYONE IN IT, JUST TO ADVANCE YOUR OWN AMBITIONS.
SPARE ME THE CIVICS LESSON AND PHILOSOPHY. I'M FIGHTING FOR MY OWN IDEALS.
AND I'M NOT ABOUT TO STOP.
GIVE UP...
HUH?!
I'LL SAY THIS JUST ONCE MORE.

YOUR FUTURE IS DEATH.
WHAT ARE YOU WAITING FOR?
PLEASE, NARUTO. KILL ME. NOW.
GASP!
!!
!

WHAT IS WITH YOU? YOU'RE USED TO BEING THE TOUGHEST. YOU DON'T LIKE TO LOSE. I GET THAT!
BUT WANTING TO DIE JUST 'CAUSE SOMEONE BEAT YOU IS CRAZY!!
...
THERE'S MORE TO LIFE THAN JUST FIGHTING. THERE'S MORE TO YOU!
YOUR BOSS MUST LIKE YOU FOR MORE THAN JUST THAT... RIGHT? DOESN'T HE?
...
THAT DAY I MET YOU IN THE FOREST... I REMEMBER THINKING THAT WE WERE TWO OF A KIND...
SURELY YOU CAN UNDER-STAND...
!
YOU'LL HAVE TO BLOODY YOUR HANDS. FORGIVE ME FOR THAT.
IS THAT...
IS THAT THE ONLY WAY? NO OTHER OUTCOME?

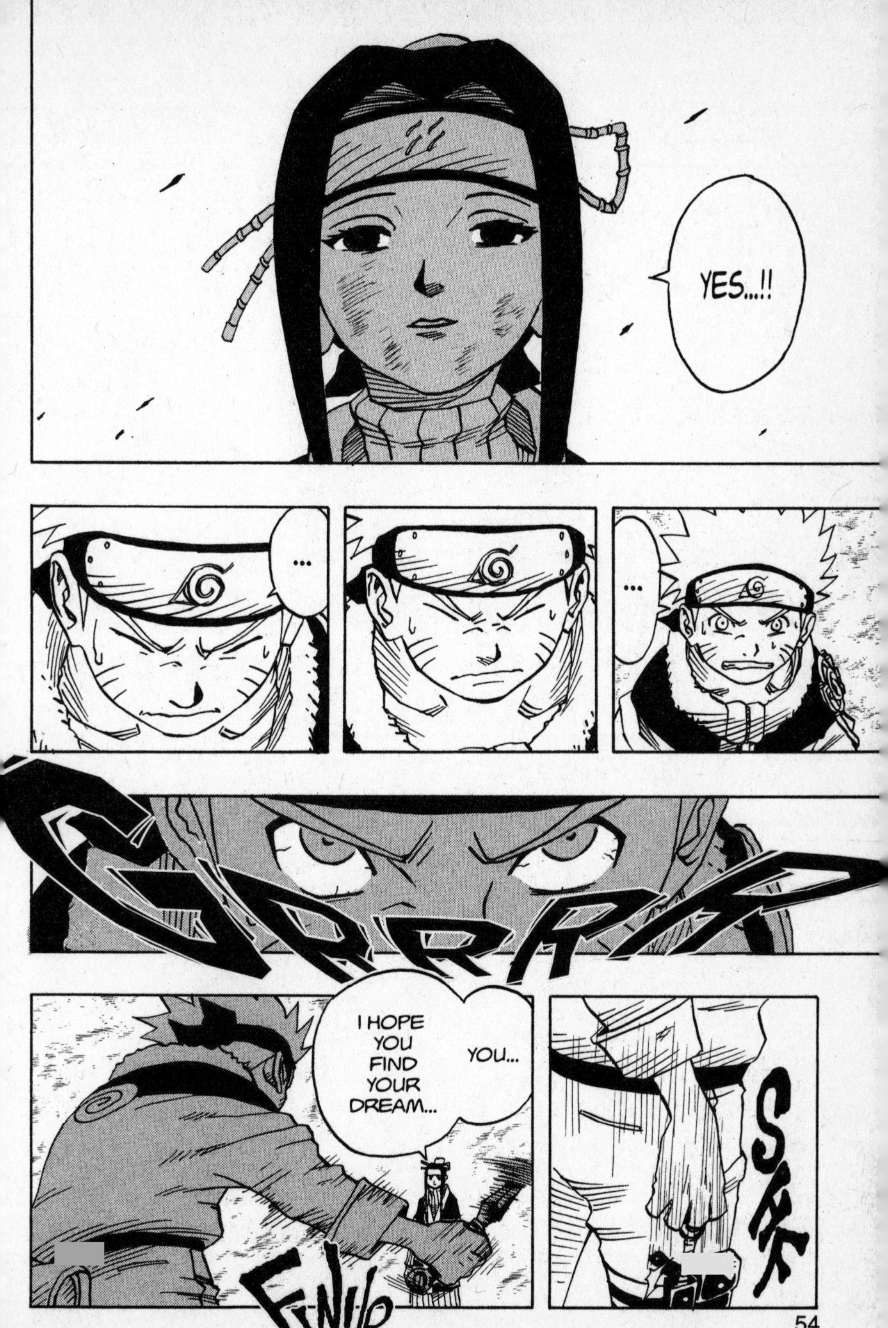
YES...!!
...
...
SRRRK
SHK
YOU...
I HOPE YOU FIND YOUR DREAM...
FWUP

...SASUKE HAD A DREAM, TOO...
...HE...
IF WE'D MET SOME OTHER WAY, SOMEPLACE ELSE, YOU AND ME'D PROBABLY HAVE BEEN FRIENDS.
CLENCH
YOU'RE GOING TO BE VERY STRONG.
THANK YOU.

THAT SUPER-THICK MIST... IT'S STARTING TO DISSIPATE...
HUH...
!
I SEE TWO PEOPLE.
BUT IT LOOKS LIKE THEY'RE JUST STANDING THERE, GLARING AT EACH OTHER...
IT'S HARD TO MAKE OUT...
WHICH ONE IS YOUR MASTER KAKASHI?
!!
OH!!
ONE OF THEM'S MOVING!!

RRRRROAR!!
!!
SHUD
DER
!!

!!
SMAP
HUNH?!
I'M SORRY, NARUTO!
FWIP
FWIP
FWIP
I CAN'T DIE YET!!
GRAB

WHAT?
!!!
DRIP
DRIP
DRIP
KLATTER
plit
plit
Plit

!!
SCHUUULGKK
AIEE!!
WH-WHAT THE-!!

SPLATTER
SPLAT
POOF
!

KOFF
!
ZABUZA... S-SIR...
!
...YOU SAID MY FUTURE WAS DEATH...
HEH HEH... BUT YOU MISSED AGAIN, KAKASHI.
SNEER

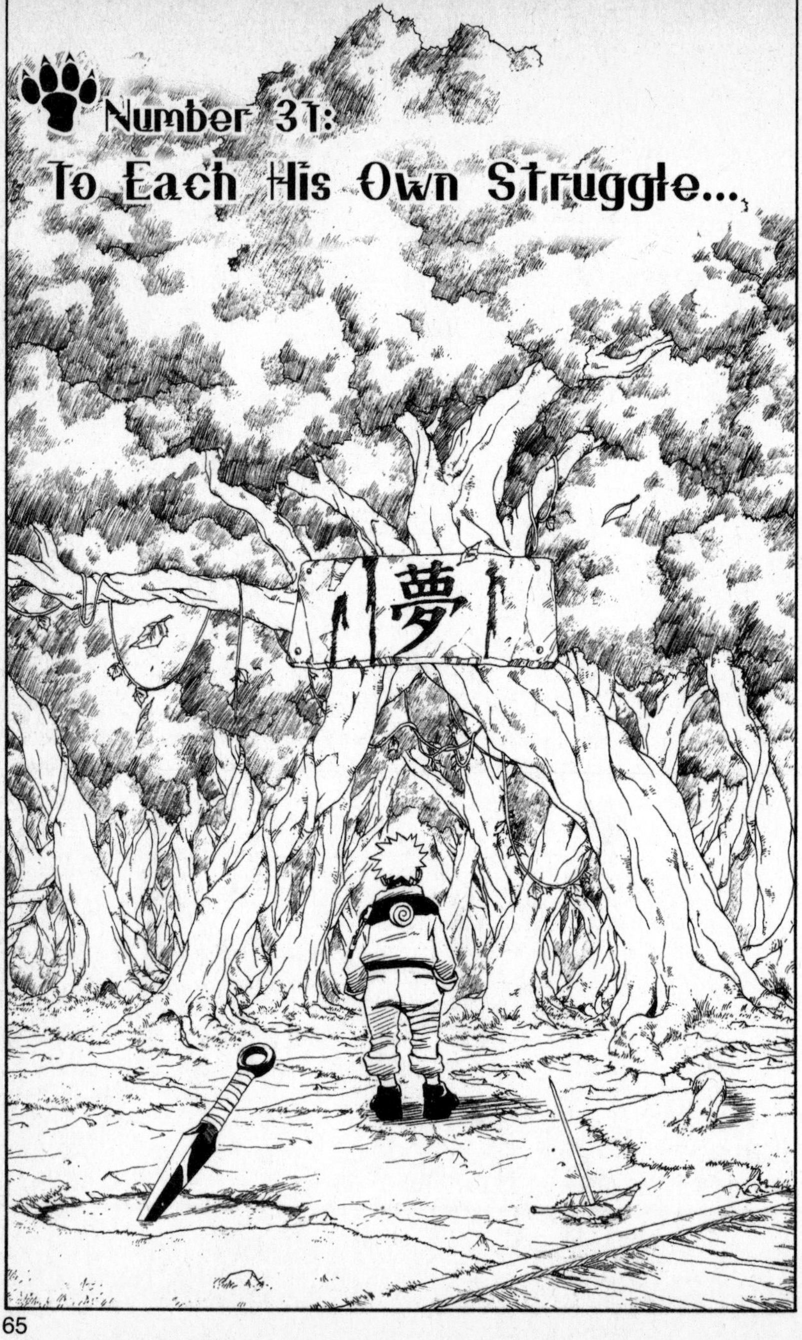

Number 31:
To Each His Own Struggle...
夢

OPEN UP! PLEASE!!!
BAM BAM
MISTER GI'ICHI!
BAM
BAM
BAM
I'M SORRY... INARI, WE'RE NOT GOING TO FIGHT BACK ANY MORE...
I NEED YOU TO COME WITH ME TO THE BRIDGE!!!
IF WE STICK TOGETHER, THIS TIME WE CAN BEAT GATô AND HIS WHOLE GANG!

YOUR FATHER...
..WAS A HERO. BUT HE'S GONE NOW.
!
IF WE FIGHT, WE'LL BE THROWING AWAY A LOT OF LIVES.
WE'VE ALREADY SACRIFICED AND LOST SO MUCH.
NONE OF US WANTS ANY MORE LOSSES... ANY MORE REGRETS.
...
...I DON'T WANT ANY REGRETS EITHER.
...
THAT'S WHY...
...I HAVE TO FIGHT.
A MAN HAS TO LIVE HIS LIFE SO THAT HE DOESN'T END UP WITH ANY REGRETS...
...I LOVE MY MA, AND GRANDPA, AND YOU...
...AND EVERY-ONE IN THE VILLAGE...
...

AND I UNDERSTAND NOW...
THAT I CAN'T PROTECT ANYONE BY BEING A BIG CRYBABY.
SKF
TAK
...
LITTLE INARI IS GROWING UP TO BE A FINE YOUNG MAN, ISN'T HE...
ARE YOU SURE HE'LL BE ALL RIGHT LIKE THAT... BY HIMSELF?
WAIT! YOU CAN'T GO TO THE BRIDGE ALONE!
HAVE TO. NO ONE IN THE VILLAGE WAS WILLING TO GO WITH ME.
BUT THAT DOESN'T MEAN...!
YANK

I MAY BE LITTLE...
...BUT I KNOW HOW TO FIGHT...
TROMP
TROMP
YOU'RE JUST A LITTLE BOY!
'CAUSE I'M MY DADDY'S SON.
...
INARI, WAIT!
KREEEEAK
!
THE MIST'S FADING... I'M SEEING THINGS MORE CLEARLY...
!
FWP
FWP
HAKU...
WHERE IS HE?!

TAK
IS THAT HIM?!
HUNH?!
WHAT... WHAT IN...?!
WH-...
!!
PUFF
HUFF
HUFF
SCHLUUGK

ISN'T THAT THAT BOY IN THE MASK...?!
HE JUMPED BETWEEN... TO SAVE ZABUZA...
CLENCH
THAT WAS BRILLIANT... HAKU.
...
HEH HEH...
...
...THE BOY...
!

...IS ALREADY...
...DEAD.
HE'S GOING TO COME RIGHT THROUGH THE KID TO GET TO ME!
KANNG

!!
MASTER KAKASHI!!
I AM YOUR WEAPON AND YOUR TOOL...
I REALLY DID FIND A TREASURE IN THAT GUTTER...
TO THINK THAT HE'D GRANT ME THIS MARVELOUS CHANCE IN THE END!!
GRAB
HOP

THAT UNFORGIVABLE SCUMBAG!
GRRR
HEH HEH... SO...YOU WERE ABLE TO GET AWAY... BECAUSE POOR HAKU WAS ALREADY DEAD.
SHF
NARUTO... STAY OUT OF THIS!
!

!
...NARUTO...?
THIS IS MY FIGHT!!
NARUTO--!!! YOU'RE ALIVE--!!
SAKURA!!

HUH?
WHAT ABOUT SASUKE?
!!
NARUTO!! WHERE'S SASUKE?!!!
FLINCH
...
?
...
...
TAK
!!
FOCUS, KAKASHI! DON'T LET YOUR-SELF BE DISTRACTED!!!

THUNK
GACK
!
TREMMBLE
...I'LL STAY WITH YOU
SO THAT YOU WON'T BE DISOBEYING YOUR MASTER'S ORDER.
...
GRIP
UH-HUHN.
TAK

!!
SKFF

HE'S SO COLD.
THIS ISN'T AN ILLUSION... IS IT...?
DON'T HOLD BACK FOR MY SAKE. THERE ARE TIMES IT'S WHEN RIGHT TO GIVE IN AND SHED SOME GOOD HONEST TEARS.
I...
... ALWAYS GOT PERFECT SCORES ON ALL MY TESTS IN SCHOOL.
!
I MEMORIZED EACH AND EVERY ONE OF THE ONE HUNDRED RULES OF CONDUCT FOR NINJA AND SHINOBI. I USED TO WRITE THEM OUT WITH PRIDE.
WE HAD A TEST ONE DAY. AND THE QUESTION WAS ...
...!
"WHAT IS THE TWENTY-FIFTH RULE OF SHINOBI CONDUCT?"
JUST LIKE ALWAYS, I WROTE IT DOWN.
?!

"NO MATTER WHAT HAPPENS, TRUE SHINOBI MUST NEVER... EVER... SHOW THEIR EMOTIONS!
"TH-THE MISSION IS THE ONLY PRIORITY. CARRY THAT IN YOUR HEART. AND NEVER, NEVER, SH-SHED A TEAR..."
DRIP
DRIP
SOB
SOB
...
SO THIS... THIS IS WHAT A SHINOBI IS... IT'S UNBEARABLE...
SASUKE...!
SOB!!
RRRR
RRR

WHY... WHY... CAN'T I KEEP UP...?
HUFF
HUFF
HUFF
HUFF
DAMN IT!!
TAK
WHOP
...!
UHN...!

WH
A
SHHF
GRAB
!!
NOW THERE'S NO WAY YOU CAN BEAT ME.
WHAT?!
IT'S OVER. YOU JUST DON'T KNOW IT YET.
HEH-HEH! I WONDER HOW THE FIGHT'S GOING!
TAP

FWUP
SMAK
!!
FWUK
32: THE TOOLS CALLED SHINOBI
THIS IS GOOD-BYE...
..."DEMON"!
SHUKK
!

!!
Number 32:
The Tools Called Shinobi

KOFF
DRIP
!
K-KLUNK
PLIT
PLIT
...
SHUDDER
NOW YOU CAN'T USE EITHER ARM.
NO SPELLS. NO KATAS. NO CHAKRA.
UHN
WELL, HE'S CERTAINLY MADE A FINE MESS OUT OF YOU!
POK
WHAT A PITY...
!

BA BAM
MUTTER
ZABUZA!
GATô...
WHAT ARE YOU... DOING HERE? AND... WHY.... DID YOU... BRING... ALL OF THEM?!
HIM...
HEH HEH HEH— THERE'S BEEN A SLIGHT CHANGE OF PLAN, ZABUZA. OR OF YOUR PLANS, ANYWAY.
—THIS WAS WHAT I HAD IN MIND ALL ALONG.
YOU MUST HAVE GUESSED. I NEVER INTENDED TO PAY YOU.
WHAT?
YOU'RE GOING TO DIE, "DEMON"... HERE AND NOW.

...IT'S SUCH A BOTHER HIRING A SKILLED SHINOBI AFFILIATED WITH ONE OF THE TOP VILLAGES. IT'S EXPENSIVE... AND THEY TEND TO HAVE FRIENDS WHO OBJECT WHEN I BETRAY AND KILL THEM.
IT'S SO MUCH SIMPLER TO HIRE *UKENIN*—RENEGADES—LIKE YOURSELF. NO ONE CARES WHAT I DO TO YOUR KIND ONCE THE JOB IS DONE.
ALL OF YOU NINJA ARE SO EAGER TO FIGHT EACH OTHER. ONCE YOU'VE WORN EACH OTHER DOWN, COMMON THUGS CAN FINISH OFF THE REST.
IT'S A GREAT BUSINESS PLAN—EFFICIENT AND INEXPENSIVE.
MY ONLY MISTAKE WAS HIRING YOU IN THE FIRST PLACE.
CALLING YOURSELF THE DEMON OF KIRIGAKURE IS JUST PLAIN FALSE ADVERTISING!
HEH HEH... YOU'RE NO DEMON...
MORE LIKE A **BABY** DEMON, IF THAT.
GAHAHAHAHAHAHA!
THE SHAPE YOU'RE IN, WE'LL TAKE YOU DOWN WITHOUT EVEN BREAKING A SWEAT!
HAHAHAHAHA
WHO THE HECK ARE THEY?
THAT'S SOME CROWD!

I NO LONGER HAVE ANY REASON TO WANT TO ASSASSINATE TAZUNA...
...WHICH SETTLES OUR DIFFERENCES.
HA HA HA
OUR FIGHT IS OVER.
FORGIVE ME... KAKASHI...
GYA
!!
HA HA HA HA HA
YOU'RE RIGHT.
GYA HA HA
HA HA HA
YEAH...
HUH?
I STILL HAVE A SCORE TO SETTLE.
!
!
...THAT REMINDS ME...
TAP
TAP
TOK
TAP
TAP

YOU... CRUSHED MY ARM UNTIL YOU ALMOST BROKE THE BONES!
POKE
WHAT THE HECK ARE YOU DOING, YOU CREEP?!
DEAD MEAT. CARRION.
KICK
HAH.
HEY, WHY DON'T YOU DO SOMETHING?! HE WORKED FOR YOU! HE WAS PRACTICALLY YOUR SLAVE!!
HEY!!
COOL DOWN. THINK. THERE'S A LOT OF THEMM.
GRAB
DASH

HE WAS YOUR COMRADE... YOUR PARTNER... HE WORKED FOR YOU FOR YEARS!!!
BUT YOU SHOULD CARE! THAT FAT SCUMBAG IS DESECRATING HIM!!!
!!
HAKU IS DEAD.
BUT...
LIKE WHAT?
I DIDN'T VALUE HAKU FOR HIMSELF... BUT FOR THE TAINT HIS BLOOD CARRIED... AND FOR WHAT HIS TALENTS COULD DO FOR ME.
I APOLOGIZE FOR NOTHING.
...GATŌ'S BEEN USING ME... AND I USED HAKU.
WEREN'T YOU LISTENING? IT'S A SHINOBI'S LOT. ALL OF US ARE EITHER USERS, OR TOOLS... OR BOTH.
STOP IT, NARUTO! LEAVE HIM ALONE. OUR QUARREL IS OVER.
!
CHFF
BESIDES WHICH...
...
YOU...
DO YOU REALLY MEAN THAT?

HE'S STILL MY ENEMY!!!
SHUT UP--!!
...
HUFF
HUFF
HUFF
HE...
HE REALLY CARED ABOUT YOU!!
WHO IS THAT OBNOXIOUS BRAT?... HE'S BEEN MAKING QUITE A NUISANCE OF HIMSELF!

DO YOU HAVE ANYONE SPECIAL IN YOUR LIFE?
HE WAS DEVOTED TO YOU!!
WHEN PEOPLE ARE PROTECTING SOMETHING TRULY PRECIOUS TO THEM...
...THEY TRULY CAN BECOME... AS STRONG AS THEY MUST BE!
...
BUT YOU THINK THAT'S JUST NOTHING, THAT HE WAS NOTHING. YOU DON'T FEEL A THING!
I...FIND IT DIFFICULT TO EMBRACE THE FULL SHINOBI PHILOSOPHY.
ARE YOU REALLY THAT HEARTLESS?
I'M WILLING TO DO WHATEVER IT TAKES... TO FULFILL THAT PERSON'S DREAMS...
TO THAT END, I WILL BECOME A TRUE SHINOBI...
IS THAT HOW YOU GET... WHEN YOUR POWERS ARE AS STRONG AS YOURS ARE?

WILLING TO DO WHATEVER IT TAKES... TO FULFILL THAT PERSON'S DREAMS...
DOING SO IS MY OWN DREAM.
HE GAVE HIS LIFE FOR YOU!
TO DIE AS HIS TOOL...
I WAS SO HAPPY...!
HE DIED... WITHOUT ANY OF HIS DREAMS EVER COMING TRUE.
PLIT
PLIT
KID.
...
THAT'S... TOO MUCH, TOO CRUEL...

...NOT...
...ANOTHER WORD.
PLIT
PLIT
...

WHAT HAKU DID... WAS NOT JUST FOR ME.
WHILE WE FOUGHT, HE BROKE HIS HEART... OVER YOU... AND YOUR FRIENDS. THAT'S THE TRUTH.
CHA
...!
KID...
YOU'RE RIGHT, YOU KNOW.
...I'M GLAD MY LAST BATTLE... WAS AGAINST YOU...BOY.
...HUH?
?!
HE WAS TOO KIND... TOO GENTLE.
BITE
SHRRRED
WOULD YOU LEND ME YOUR KUNAI KNIFE?
FLUTTER
...
!
AND I'VE LOST... EVERYTHING.
SAY WHAT WE WILL, DO WHAT WE WILL. IN THE END, WE SHINOBI ARE STILL JUST PEOPLE AFTER ALL... WITH FEELINGS ALL-TOO-HUMAN.
HUNH? UH...
!!
SURE.

CHUCK
TIK
WHAT?!
THAT'S ENOUGH! WHAT ARE YOU WAITING FOR? KILL ALL OF THEM!
THOP
THOP
LET'S GO!
YEAH!!
TOK TOK TOK
EVEN IF YOU'RE A NINJA, YOU'RE HALF-DEAD, AGAINST ALL OF US!
YOU DON'T STAND A CHANCE!

!
A...
A DEMON!!

CHOK-CHOK-CHOK
CHOK
CHUKKK
WHY WON'T YOU DIE?!

I-IF YOU'RE IN SUCH A HURRY... TO BE REUNITED WITH YOUR LITTLE FRIEND... GO ALONE!
I... HAVE NO INTENTION... OF GOING TO THE SAME PLACE... AS HAKU...
WH-WHAT ARE YOU BABBLING ABOUT?
UGH...
HEH...
...I'M TAKING YOU WITH ME...
...TO HELL!!
EVEN AN OGRE IN NAME ONLY... A WASHOUT FROM KIRIGAKURE VILLAGE... CAN BECOME A REAL DEMON IN HOW HE MEETS HIS DEATH.
SPLURT
AHH--!
AIEEE--!
ONCE WE'RE IN HELL, I CAN TAKE MY TIME, AND SHOW YOU OVER... AND OVER... WHO IS, OR IS NOT, "A BABY DEMON"!
!!
SHUF

WHOK
AUUGH!!
THOP
THOP
THUD
GULP
...

GRGRRR
EEEEK!!
PLEASE... KEEP ME BESIDE YOU...
STUMBLE
IT'S... GOODBYE NOW, HAKU...
THANKS FOR EVERYTHING...
AND I'M SORRY...

KISHIMOTO MASASHI'S THIRD MANGA REJECT SPECIAL!

ONCE AGAIN, THE ROUGH SKETCH TO THE LEFT IS FROM ANOTHER REJECTED MANGA. IT WAS A BASEBALL MANGA, TITLED SIMPLY "BASEBALL KING." I PLAYED BASEBALL MYSELF, BACK IN MY STUDENT DAYS, SO I (MAYBE FOOLISHLY) THOUGHT I WOULD TRY MY HAND AT A BASEBALL STORY.

DURING THIS PERIOD, I WAS IN A SITUATION WHERE, NO MATTER HOW MANY CONCEPTS FOR ADVENTURE MANGA I SKETCHED OUT, I DIDN'T GET ANY GREEN LIGHTS, SO I THOUGHT I SHOULD GO FOR A SPORTS THEME.

BUT WHEN I ACTUALLY TRIED TO DRAW ONE, PERHAPS BECAUSE I WAS WRITING FROM PERSONAL EXPERIENCE, IT BECAME A MORE REALISTIC WORK THAN I HAD INTENDED.

THE REASON IT FAILED WAS THAT IT WAS TOO SERIOUS FOR A SHONEN PUBLICATION. IT WASN'T ENTERTAINMENT.

HOWEVER, "BASEBALL KING" ACTUALLY STILL HOLDS A SPECIAL PLACE IN MY HEART. I SOMETIMES FIND MYSELF THINKING, "THAT WAS SO FUNNY... I CAN'T BELIEVE IT'S A REJECT, DARN IT...!"

33: THE BRIDGE OF THE HERO!!
THIS WAS THE END OF A MAN WHO LIVED FULL OUT.
DON'T LOOK AWAY.
YEAH...
...
SOB
AM I... AM I...?!
SAKURA...?!
SOB
SOB
SOB
AM I... DEAD...?
SASUKE...
LUB-DUP
SOB
SOB

Number 33:
The Bridge of The Hero!!
...SAKURA...
YOUR ARM'S HEAVY...

...?
...!!
OHHHHH!!
GRAB
!
SASUKE!!!!
SASUKE!
SASUKE!!
SNIFF
SOB
DRIP
DRIP
SNIFF
...
SAKURA... YOU'RE HURTING ME...
OH!
S- SORRY...
I'M SO HAPPY FOR YOU, SAKURA.

!!
...I'M ALL RIGHT... HOW'S NARUTO?
AND THAT... LITTLE CREEP IN THE MASK... WHAT HAPPENED TO HIM?
DON'T TRY TO MOVE!
NARUTO'S FINE! AND THE BOY IN THE MASK IS DEAD...
!!
DID NARUTO...? DEAD--?!
N-NO...
I MEAN... I'M NOT SURE. I DIDN'T SEE IT VERY WELL. BUT THE BOY DIED TRYING TO PROTECT ZABUZA.
...
HMM.
I... WAS AFRAID.... I THOUGHT...
I'M SO GLAD...
YOU'RE AMAZING, SASUKE. YOU SURVIVED A DEATHBLOW.
...
NO...

NOT ME. HIM.
...HE NEVER PLANNED TO... FROM THE START...
!
NARUTO--!!
SAKURA?!!
HUNH?
IT'S SASUKE. HE'S ALL RIGHT!!
HE'S ALIVE!!
--!!
...
...
...
HEH... HEH...

I GET IT... HE....
HE WAS TOO KIND... TOO GENTLE.
HAKU ....WHILE WE FOUGHT, HE BROKE HIS HEART... OVER YOU... AND YOUR FRIENDS. THAT'S THE TRUTH.
¡SASUKE!!!
SASUKE MADE IT AFTER ALL. FANTASTIC!
I'VE BEEN WORRYING SINCE THE FIGHT BEGAN... BUT...
!!
!
HEY!
AREN'T YOU SWEET-HEARTS FORGETTING SOMETHING?!
THOP
RATTLE

YOU NINJA KILLED OUR MEAL TICKET!
AND NOW YOU'RE GONNA DIE!!!
THE ONLY WAY WE CAN EVEN BREAK EVEN NOW...
...IS TO OVERRUN THE CITY AND LOOT EVERY BUSINESS AND HOME!!
OH YEAH!
K-CHK
K-CHK
CHAAAARGE
LET'S GO!
UHHH... THIS ISN'T GOOD.
MASTER KAKASHI— ISN'T THERE SOME TECHNIQUE WE CAN USE TO TAKE THEM ALL DOWN AT ONCE?
I'M AFRAID ... WITH THE LIGHTNING BLADE, THE ILLUSIONS AND CONJURATIONS... FOR THE MOMENT, I'VE EXHAUSTED MY CHAKRA.
SHUUP
!!
HEYY--!
SKID
STEP
STUMBLE
THUKK
!?

STOP WHERE YOU ARE.
THIS ISLAND IS OUR HOME. ONE STEP FURTHER...
YOU'LL DIE WHERE YOU STAND!
...
INARI...
ALL OF YOU...
INARI!!
HEH HEH.
IT'S BEING A HERO, YOU KNOW? ALL THAT NICK OF TIME STUFF!

ONNNG
ART OF THE SHADOW DOPPLE-GANGER!!
FWUP
GOOD ONE, KID. MIND IF I JOIN IN?
FLIP
BUT A BLUFF SHOULD BE ENOUGH FOR THESE BOZOS!
FWUP
I CAN'T MANAGE ANYTHING SOLID WITH MY CHAKRA SO LOW.
YIPE!

KAKASHI STYLE
ART OF THE SHADOW DOPPLE-GANGER!!
AIEE--!!!
NOW... SHALL WE?!

TAK TAKTAKTAK
RUN AWAY!!!
NEVER MIND!!
WOO-HOO!!!
YAY..!!
SPLASH
SPLASH
YAAGH--!
SKF
POOF
POOF
POOF
...LOOKS LIKE IT'S ALL OVER...
...EH, KAKASHI?
YEAH.

KAKASHI... DO ME A FAVOR?
WHAT IS IT?
...I WANT TO...
...SEE... HIS FACE.
...
YANK
SURE.
SHF
HUH?
...
IT'S SNOWING.

ARE YOU CRYING?
MY DEAR HAKU...
IN THE MIDDLE OF SUMMER...?
YOU WERE AT MY SIDE RIGHT FROM THE START...
AND I'M AT YOURS, NOW, AT THE END...
...THANK YOU ... KAKASHI.
...IF I COULD... ...IF I WERE ABLE... I WOULD WANT TO GO... TO THE SAME PLACE... ON THE OTHER SIDE ...
...AS YOU.

PLIT
YOU CAN GO WITH HIM, ZABUZA...
...GO TO THAT PLACE... TOGETHER.
...HE...WAS BORN IN A VILLAGE WHERE IT SNOWS A LOT...
SOB!
I SEE...
HE WAS A PURE SPIRIT - AS TRUE AND CLEAN AS A NEWLY FALLEN SNOW.

TWO WEEKS LATER
GRAB
OWW!
HACK
WHAT SNEAKY, GREEDY TRICK ARE YOU UP TO NOW?
GRRR
HEH HEH
YOU EAT AN OFFERING, YOU'LL BE PUNISHED BY THE GODS!
...
BUT STILL...
MASTER KAKASHI...
HMM--?
...I CAN'T HELP WONDERING. WERE THOSE TWO RIGHT ABOUT WHAT A NINJA SHOULD BE?
A SHINOBI SHOULDN'T BE CONCERNED WITH A REASON FOR HER OWN EXISTENCE...
IT IS IMPORTANT MERELY THAT WE EXIST AS A TOOL FOR OUR HOMELAND TO USE IN WHATEVER WAY THEY NEED.
THAT'S AS TRUE FOR US IN KONOHAGAKURE AS IT FOR NINJA ANYWHERE ELSE.
...
IS THAT REALLY WHAT BECOMING A FULL-FLEDGED NINJA'S GONNA BE ABOUT?
I DON'T LIKE THE SOUND OF IT!

DO YOU REALLY FEEL THAT WAY, MASTER KAKASHI?
WELLL... NO.
AND THAT'S WHY ALL WE NINJA LIVE OUR LIVES WITH THAT IDEAL ALWAYS BUBBLING BENEATH THE SURFACE OF OUR MINDS, DISTURBING US.
...LIKE IT DID ZABUZA...
AND THE BOY...
...
THAT'S IT. I'VE MADE UP MY MIND!
I AM GOING TO CREATE MY OWN *NINDO*—MY OWN NINJA PATH. MY OWN DESTINY!
!

THANKS TO YOU, OUR BRIDGE HAS FINALLY BEEN COMPLETED, BUT...
IT'S GOING TO BE AWFULLY DULL AROUND HERE, ONCE YOU'RE GONE.
WE'VE ENJOYED YOUR HOSPITALITY.
NO PROBLEMO, TAZUNA, MY MAN!! WE'LL COME BACK TO PLAY WITH YOU AGAIN SOMETIME!
PAT
YOU BETTER...
TREMBLE
...AW...
LUB-DUP
SO... UM... ANYWAY...
...
I'M NOT GONNA CRY!!
B-BUT NARUTO... HEY, "BIG BROTHER" ... Y-YOU CAN CRY! GO AHEAD!
ME? NO WAY.
FWUP
SEE YOU.
INARI... DON'T LET IT GET YOU DOWN.
IT'S OKAY TO CRY, IF YOU REALLY WANT!
...
OH!

BONEHEADS!
SOB!
BLUBBER
AND THERE'S ONLY NAME THAT WILL TRULY FIT.
AND SPEAKING OF BRIDGES, WE STILL HAVE TO OFFICIALLY DEDICATE THIS ONE.
WHAT ARE GOING TO CALL IT?
NARUTO BUILT THE BRIDGE THAT EVENTUALLY CARRIED US ALL TO HOPE AND COURAGE!
THAT BOY TOUCHED LITTLE INARI'S HEART... AND INARI TOUCHED THE HEARTS OF ALL THE PEOPLE IN OUR CITY...
HOW ABOUT... THE GREAT NARUTO BRIDGE?

HEE HEE... IT'S A NICE NAME, DAD.
ALL RIGHT--! LET'S GET HOME. MASTER IRUKA'S GONNA TAKE ME OUT FOR RAMEN NOODLES TO CELEBRATE US ACCOMPLISHING OUR MISSION!
AND THEN... AND THEN, YOU KNOW, I HAVE TO TELL LITTLE KONOHAMARU MY EPIC TALE OF MARTIAL ARTS BRAVERY--!!
OH... UH... OKAY. BY THE WAY, SASUKE... WHEN WE DO GET HOME... WOULD YOU LIKE TO... GO OUT WITH ME?
UH, NO. THANKS.
N-NO...?...
HEY! I'LL GO OUT WITH YOU!
NARUTO! NO! KNOCK IT OFF!
ARE YOU SURE? CALLING IT THAT...?!
HEH... QUITE SURE. YOU SEE, I HOPE THAT IN GIVING IT THAT NAME, WE'LL ENSURE THAT IT WILL STAND FOREVER...
OUR BRIDGE WILL BECOME SUPER-FAMOUS THE WORLD OVER, AS A SYMBOL OF TRIUMPH AND ENDURANCE!
THAT'S WHAT I HOPE... AND HOPEFULLY, THAT'S HOW IT'LL BE.

Number 34: Intruders?

YAAAAAAWN
MILK
RAMEN
YAK PAK
MUNCH
MUNCH
GLUG
GLUG
POK
HEH
WOO-HOO! NO MATTER WHAT TODAY'S MISSION IS, I'LL HAVE THE ENERGY TO FACE IT NOW!
TAK
START YOUR ENGINES!! MACH 5!!

GOOD MORNING, SAKURAAAA!!
OH!
...
HMMF!
...
...
SKF
!
SKID
!
...
DIE, FREAKS!
INNER SAKURA
?
NOT AGAIN!
EVER SINCE WE GOT HOME FROM THE LAND OF WAVES, THESE TWO HAVE BEEN ACTING JUST PLAIN WEIRD!
IT'S SOOO EMBARRASSING!
ANY TIME NOW, MASTER KAKASHI! HURRY UUUUP!!

THREE HOURS LATER...
GOOD MORNING, EVERYONE.
I'M AFRAID I GOT LOST ON THE WAY HERE...
YOUR NOSE IS GROWING, MASTER!!!
YOU ALWAYS LAY IT ON TOO THICK.
AS NINJA DECEPTIONS GO... THAT ONE SUCKS!
HOT NEW SHOW!
PREMIERE!
HEY, MASTER KAKASHI! ANY HOT NEW MISSIONS FOR THE 7TH CELL? WE'VE HAD NOTHING BUT GIMMES! BORRRRING!
SIZZLE
WE WANT ACTION! A CHALLENGE! SOMETHING WHERE I COULD USE MY SKILL -LIKE THIS... AND THIS... AND - AND -
OH, REALLY?
I SEE WHERE YOU'RE GOING WITH THIS...
GRR... THOSE TWO...
EVERY TIME WE GO ON A MISSION, THEY END UP SHOWING ME UP AND SAVING ME. BUT NOT THIS TIME!
DOPE.
GKA
IT'S OVER, AS OF NOW!
WHEW
GASP!
HUFF
PUFF
SAVING YOU IS SUCH A NUISANCE, SASUKE!
THAT'S WHAT I'LL TELL 'IM!!
TAK
HEY, NARUTO! WAKE UP! WE'RE HEADING OUT ON OUR MISSION!
YESSIR!
WOULD YOU CHILL?!

OPENS TODAY
AT LAST IT COMES TO LIFE! NEW MAKE-OUT PARADISE
AND AT THE MISSION'S END...
THROB
SIGH...
THROB
YOU'D HAVE BEEN FINE IF YOU HADN'T OVERDONE IT.
YOU'RE A REAL NUISANCE.
THAT DOES IT!! SASUKE·
IF YOU START ANYTHING MORE, I'LL BURY YOU!
...
HAH!
!
SNAP
FLINCH
YOU TELL HIM! YOU'RE ALWAYS MESSING UP OUR TEAMWORK, SASUKE!!
HE WAS TALKING TO YOU, PINHEAD.
IF YOU'RE SO SICK OF BEING IN MY DEBT...
LATELY... YOUR TEAMWORK HAS BEEN ALMOST NON-EXISTENT.
HMM...

!!
WHY DON'T YOU...
GET BETTER THAN ME?
I HATE THIS... THERE ARE GUYS OUT THERE WHO COULD CHALLENGE ME, BUT I'M STUCK ON NOTHING ASSIGNMENTS WITH THIS TWERP.
BITE
I DON'T KNOW HOW THEY MANAGED IT, BUT THEY'RE ON EVEN WORSE TERMS NOW THAN THEY WERE BEFORE.
!
BOP
FLIP
SKREE
SKREE

OKAY, THAT'S IT. WE'LL CALL IT A DAY RIGHT NOW.
I'VE GOT TO GO HAND IN MY REPORT ON TODAY'S MISSION.
THEN I'M GOING HOME.
SHHHF
!
OH!
HEY! SASUKE, WAIT UP!
...
I... I WAS WONDERING... IF... ♡
AW, MAN!!!
IF WE, YOU KNOW... YOU AND I... JUST THE TWO OF US... COULD WORK ON OUR, UM... OUR ♡ TEAMWORK?
YOU'RE AS BAD AS NARUTO.
WHY WASTE YOUR TIME FLIRTING WHEN YOU SHOULD BE PRACTICING?
LIKE NARUTO!
INNER SAKURA
THUNK
EVEN HIS SKILLS ARE BETTER THAN YOURS!
WORSE THAN NARUTO!
NO WAY!!!
INNER SAKURA!!
THUNK
THUD

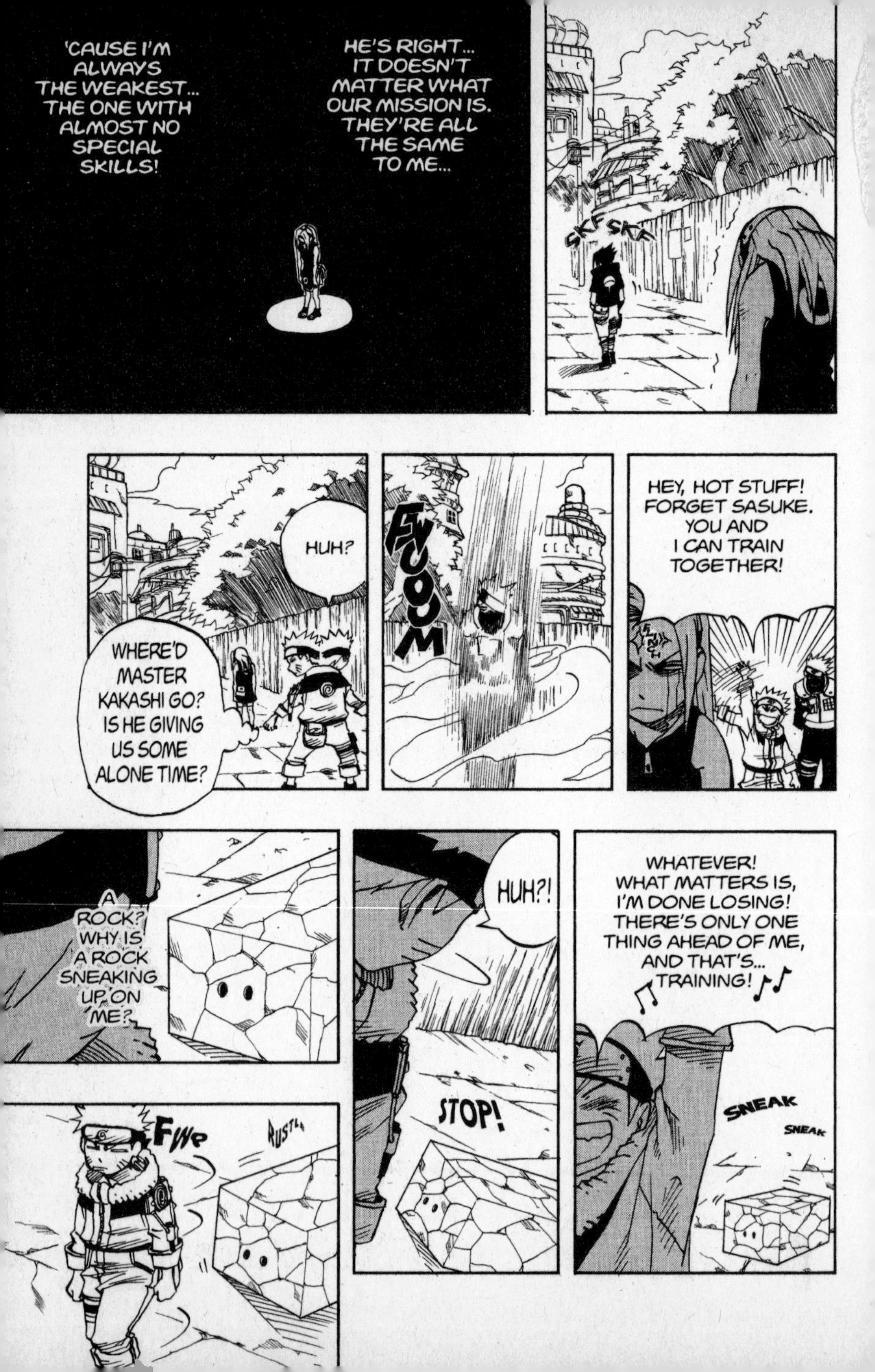
'CAUSE I'M ALWAYS THE WEAKEST... THE ONE WITH ALMOST NO SPECIAL SKILLS!
HE'S RIGHT... IT DOESN'T MATTER WHAT OUR MISSION IS. THEY'RE ALL THE SAME TO ME...
SKF SKF
HUH?
WHERE'D MASTER KAKASHI GO? IS HE GIVING US SOME ALONE TIME?
FWOOM
HEY, HOT STUFF! FORGET SASUKE. YOU AND I CAN TRAIN TOGETHER!
A ROCK? WHY IS A ROCK SNEAKING UP ON ME?
HUH?!
WHATEVER! WHAT MATTERS IS, I'M DONE LOSING! THERE'S ONLY ONE THING AHEAD OF ME, AND THAT'S... TRAINING!
STOP!
SNEAK
SNEAK

LITTLE HINT... NO ROCK HAS PERFECT ANGLES, PERFECT CORNERS... AND EYE HOLES. KIND OF A BIG CLUE.
YIPE
RATTLE
OW!
FWP
PSYCH!! FAKED YOU OUT, ROCK!!!
TA-DAAAA
LEAVE IT TO THE MAN I HAVE ACKNOWLEDGED AS BEING ALMOST MY EQUAL! YOUR SKILLS RIVAL MY OWN!!
OOF
GRUNT
...
HEH HEH HEH
YOU'RE OUR IDOL, RIGHT? WE'RE COPYING THE STYLE YOU USED TO WEAR.
UHHH...
WHAT'S UP WITH THE GOGGLES?
OH, IT'S YOU GUYS.

OH-KAAAAAY....
WHAT DO YOU MEAN, "OKAY?"
SUDDENLY TOO COOL FOR SCHOOL, BIG GUY?
!
WHAT DO YOU WANT FROM ME?
WE'LL SHOW YOU, BOSS! CAN YOU COME NOW?
HE'S LOOKING DOWN ON US!
NOPE!
I HAVE TO TRAIN!
FWUP
BUT... BUT YOU PROMISED TO PLAY NINJA WITH US!! RIGHT?
HEH... OH, YEAH... WAS THAT TODAY?
IF I PLAY WITH THEM, EVEN A LITTLE, THEY'LL WASTE MY WHOLE DAY!
SO... JUST WHAT IS A NINJA DOING "PLAYING NINJA", HMM?
DUM DUM DOM
TAK TAK
...

!
GRR
BUT WHO AM I TO TALK? I'M WORSE THAN HE IS!
UH, YES? CAN WE HELP YOU?
HEY, BIG GUY, WHO'S THE BABE?
THE WAY SHE'S LOOKING AT ME... STOP! I'M BLUSHING!!
THAT CHICK'S EYING HIM LIKE SHE'D LIKE TO KILL HIM AND DEVOUR HIS CORPSE!
HEY, BIG GUY, SEEING AS HOW YOU'RE SO SMART AND SUAVE AND ALL...
BOFF
HUNH?
THE HOTTIE... I CAN TELL... YOU AND SHE ARE......
...YOU KNOWWWW! RIGHT?
WINK
!!

HEH HEH HEH
FOR LITTLE GUYS, YOU CATCH ON QUICK.
WRONG!!!
POW
WHO
THUMP
SKID
BIG GUY!!
BAM
(HUFF) (PUFF) (PUFF)
WH-WHAT DID YOU DO THAT FOR?!
YOU'RE OUR LEADER! YOU CAN'T DIE!
YOU TOTAL WITCH!
INNER SAKURA
LEMME AT 'IM!
CRUNCH

THANKS FOR YOUR LATEST REPORT, MASTER KAKASHI.
...
HOW'S OUR LITTLE HELLION?
DOES HE GET ALONG WELL WITH THE OTHER MEMBERS OF HIS CELL?
HE'S... GETTING THERE.
YOUR TEAM'S SEEN A LOT OF ACTION LATELY.
NARUTO HASN'T HAD TIME TO GET TOGETHER WITH ME ONCE. I CAN'T HELP WORRYING ABOUT HIM.
SCRATCH
YOU KNOW HOW IT IS, MASTER IRUKA. UCHIHA SASUKE IS IN OUR CELL, TOO. HE AND NARUTO ARE LIKE A COUPLE OF DOGS, ALWAYS CIRCLING EACH OTHER, SNAPPING AND SNARLING.
BUT IT KEEPS NARUTO ON HIS TOES. HE'S DEVELOPING FAST. HE'S ALWAYS HOPING TO CATCH UP TO HIS HERO... **YOU.**
...!
REALLY?

KONOHAMARU! ARE YOU ALL RIGHT?
HMF
STOMP
STOMP
!!
...JEESH! THAT BROAD-BROWED, FIREBREATHING HAG! IS SHE EVEN A REAL FEMALE?!
OWW
HUNH?!
RUUUUUN
ARRRRRGH!!
YIPE!

OOOONG
THAT'S GOTTA SMART!
!!

TUHTWEEET
NOW WHAT?
!
HUFF
HUFF
HUFF
NOW'S THE TIME!
MUNCH

UNNH...
THAT HURT, SNOTFACE!
KONOHA-MARU!!
WHO ARE THESE PEOPLE?
IT WAS MY FAULT. I WAS FOOLING AROUND...
KNOCK IT OFF. YOU'RE GONNA GET IT AS IT IS!
THESE GUYS MUST BE GENIN - JUNIOR-LEVEL NINJA - FROM KONOHA VILLAGE!
PUT HIM DOWN, YOU BIG APE!!

I JUST WANT TO PLAY WITH HIM A LITTLE... WHILE WE'RE WAITING FOR THE NUISANCE TO GET HERE!
OWW!
KRUNCH
YOU SONOFA-
ZOOM
GRRR
FLIP
GAAH!!
TRIP
?
WHAT THE HECK WAS THAT?!
WHAT A WIMP!
IS THAT THE BEST KONOHA'S *GENIN* CAN DO?!
TH- THEY'RE FOREIGNERS!
WHY ARE THEY HERE?

SEEING WHOM I INVITED HERE, YOU MAY BE ABLE TO GUESS...
...WHAT WE ARE HERE TO DISCUSS.
IS IT TIME ALREADY?
HAVE YOU INFORMED THE LORDS OF THE OTHER LANDS YET?
BECAUSE I BELIEVE I HAVE ALREADY SEEN SOME OF THEM IN OUR VILLAGE.
WHEN IS IT TO BE?
ONE WEEK FROM TODAY.
ISN'T THIS RATHER SUDDEN?
HUMF
TO MAKE IT COMPLETELY OFFICIAL, I HEREBY ANNOUNCE...
SEVEN DAYS FROM NOW, ON JULY 1ST...
WE SHALL BEGIN CONDUCTING EXAMINATIONS FOR JOURNEYMEN NINJA - THE *CHŪNIN*.

Number 35:
Iruka vs. Kakashi

KONOHA-MARU!!
KONOHA-MARU!!
...
HEY! YOU IN THE BLACK PIG SUIT!!
RELEASE HIM NOW AND I'LL GO EASY ON YOU, BONEHEAD!!
YOU'RE THE BONEHEAD!
CHOKE
DO YOU WANT THAT GUY TO KICK URANUS?!
GACK!!
YOU'RE STARTING TO ANNOY ME!
!

!!
WHAT?!
I... WILL NOT BE HELD RESPONSIBLE FOR THIS...
GASP
GUK
FIRST OFF, I'M ALLERGIC TO "SHRIMP"!
BAD ENOUGH THAT YOU'RE A SHORT LITTLE KID... YOU'RE DISRESPECTING YOUR ELDERS! YOU MAKE ME WANT TO KILL HIM!
!!
SHHK
CRUNCH
♥ SO I'LL FINISH WITH THIS TINY SHRIMP... AND MOVE ON TO THE JUMBO SHRIMP OVER THERE.
WHO IS HE? THIS IS SO NOT GOOD!
YOU•
FWIP
YOU... YOU...
THWIP

UGH!
AAGH!
THOK
TELL ME... WHAT ARE YOU GUYS DOING IN OUR VILLAGE?
HMM... PRETTY COOL!
SO?
IT'S SASUKE !!

NOW, THEN...
WE'D LIKE TO HEAR FIRST FROM THOSE WHO HAVE OVERSEEN THE TRAINING OF OUR NEWEST JUNIOR NINJA.
TAK
MASTERS KAKASHI, KURENAI, AND ASUMA.
TELL US...
...DO ANY OF YOU HAVE, AMONG YOUR CHARGES, ANY *GENIN* YOU'D RECOMMEND FOR THIS YEAR'S JOURNEYMEN EXAMS?

...THAT BEFORE WE CAN EVEN CONSIDER THEM,
THEY MUST HAVE COMPLETED A MINIMUM OF EIGHT MISSIONS.
BEYOND THAT, EMPLOY YOUR OWN JUDGMENT AS TO WHETHER THEY ARE READY TO ASPIRE TO THE NEXT LEVEL.
TO BE TRULY COMPETITIVE, CANDIDATES SHOULD PROBABLY HAVE COMPLETED AT LEAST DOUBLE THE RECOMMENDED NUMBER OF MISSIONS...
HE SHOULDN'T BE ASKING THIS YET.... IT'S TOO SOON FOR **ANY** OF THEM.
YOU MAY BEGIN, KAKASHI.
CELL NUMBER 7, LED BY KAKASHI, CONSISTS OF UCHIHA SASUKE, UZUMAKI NARUTO, AND HARUNO SAKURA. I VOW UPON THE HONOR OF MY CLAN, THE HATAKE -
- THAT ALL THREE OF THEM ARE READY FOR THE *CHŪNIN* SELECTION EXAM.

CELL NUMBER 8, LED BY KURENAI, CONSISTS OF HYUGA HINATA, INUZUKA KIBA, AND ABURAME SHINO. I VOW UPON MY OWN CLAN, THE YUHI, THAT I AM AS CERTAIN AS IS MY ESTEEMED COLLEAGUE -
- THAT ALL THREE ARE READY FOR THE *CHÛNIN* SELECTION EXAM.
WHAT?!
CELL NUMBER 10, LED BY ASUMA, CONSISTS OF YAMANAKA INO, NARA SHIKAMARU, AND AKIMICHI CHOJI. I VOW UPON MY CLAN, THE SARUTOBI, THAT I AM EQUALLY AS CERTAIN -
- THAT ALL THREE ARE READY FOR THE *CHÛNIN* SELECTION EXAM.
HOW UNUSUAL FOR ALL THREE OF YOU TO HAVE UNHESITATINGLY ASSENTED...
LORD HOKAGE!
PLEASE ALLOW ME TO SPEAK!!
YES, IRUKA?
J-JUST A MOMENT!!

FORGIVE ME IF I OVERSTEP, BUT MOST OF THE NINE STUDENTS JUST NAMED...
... WERE MY STUDENTS WHILE THEY WERE AT THE ACADEMY.
CERTAINLY, THEY ARE ALL GIFTED AND SHOW BOTH COMMITMENT AND TALENT... BUT IT'S TOO SOON FOR KIDS THAT YOUNG TO BE STEPPING UP TO THE JOURNEYMAN LEVEL.
ONLY WITH TIME WILL THEY HAVE THE KIND OF EXPERIENCE AND MATURITY THOSE EXAMS REQUIRE.
I DON'T UNDERSTAND WHY THEIR SUPERVISORS CAN'T SEE THAT.
I WAS SIX YEARS YOUNGER THAN NARUTO WHEN I ATTAINED THE RANK OF *CHÛNIN,* IRUKA.
NARUTO'S NOT LIKE YOU!
DO YOU WANT TO DESTROY THOSE CHILDREN?!
YOU ALL KNOW WHAT THEY CALL THE *CHÛNIN* SELECTION EXAMS, DON'T YOU?
THEY GRIPE ABOUT EVERY DETAIL OF EVERY MISSION. JUST FOR ONCE, I THINK IT WOULD DO THEM GOOD TO FIND OUT WHAT REAL PAIN IS...
LET'S ADMIT IT. BREAKING THEM WOULD BE FUN.
ARE YOU OUT OF YOUR MIND?

...IT WAS A JOKE, MASTER IRUKA.
I UNDERSTAND YOU... AND I'M SORRY IF MY RECOMMENDATION UPSETS YOU. BUT I STAND BY IT.
BUT...
KAKASHI... CAN WE FINISH WITH THIS?
IT'S NONE OF YOUR BUSINESS, ANYWAY...
...THEY'RE NOT YOUR STUDENTS ANYMORE.
THEY ARE SOLDIERS UNDER MY COMMAND.
...
WHAT A PEST.
...

TAK
OH, LOOK. ANOTHER LITTLE BRAT.
GET LOST.
NARUTO.... YOU SUCK!
I CAN'T BELIEVE WE LOOKED UP TO YOU!
OOO... HOW COOL!!

HE DID IT AGAIN - STICKING HIS NOSE IN AND MAKING ME LOOK BAD!!
DON'T BE STUPID. I COULD HAVE HANDLED THAT LOSER IF SASUKE HADN'T BUTTED IN!
RIIIGHT.
SHF
THINK YOU'RE PRETTY SMART, DON'T YOU?
COME DOWN, LITTLE SQUIRREL!
KANKURO! DON'T!
FWUP
TELL ME YOU'RE NOT PLANNING TO USE THE 'CROW!
TOK
!!

: GAARA'S TATTOO SAYS "LOVE."

G-
GAA-
RA...
HE...
HE SNUCK
UP BESIDE
ME...
I DIDN'T
EVEN
HAVE A
CLUE!
HIS
STEALTH
SKILLS
RIVAL
KAKASHI'S.
IT
ANNOYS
ME THAT
YOU'D LOSE
CONTROL IN
A QUARREL
WITH
CHILDREN!
HAVE
YOU
FORGOTTEN
WHY
WE
CAME
HERE?
BUT
GAARA...
THEY
STARTED IT.
THE
LITTLE
ONE
SLAMMED
ME!

SHUT UP...
OR I'LL KILL YOU.
SHIVER
YOU'RE RIGHT. I WAS OUT OF LINE.
WE'RE SORRY... OKAY, GAARA?
REALLY, REALLY SORRY!
SO HE'S IN CHARGE, EH?
HE GLARES LIKE A BASILISK.
SORRY ABOUT MY FRIENDS.
!!
FWP
THIS IS THE ONE WHO NAILED KANKURO WITH A STONE. THAT TOOK SKILL.

!
I KNOW WE'RE A LITTLE EARLY...
SHHM
... BUT WE DIDN'T COME HERE TO PLAY AROUND.
I SWEAR IT WON'T HAPPEN AGAIN.
LET'S GO.
WAIT!
!
YES?
ACCORDING TO YOUR HEADBANDS, YOU THREE...
...COME FROM THE VILLAGE HIDDEN IN THE SAND.
YOUR COUNTRY IS ONE OF KONOHA'S ALLIES...
...BUT ACCORDING TO OUR TREATY, YOUR NINJA ARE NOT PERMITTED TO CROSS THE BORDER WITHOUT AUTHORIZATION.
STATE YOUR BUSINESS!
WE CAN'T JUST LET YOU GO YOUR MERRY WAY.

...EVER HEARD THE OLD SAYING ABOUT IT BEING DARKEST AT THE BASE OF THE BRIGHTEST LIGHT-HOUSE?
WEREN'T YOU INFORMED?
TA-DA! MY TRAVEL PAPERS!
!
AS YOU GUESSED, WE'RE JUNIOR-LEVEL NINJA FROM THE HIDDEN SAND VILLAGE.
WE'RE HERE TO TAKE THE *CHÛNIN* SELECTION EXAM
...
WHAT'S THE *CHÛNIN* SELECTION EXAM?
YOU REALLY DON'T KNOW? JUNIOR NINJA ARE SENT FROM THE HIDDEN SAND VILLAGE AND THE MINOR LANDS BETWEEN OUR HOME AND YOURS TO COMPETE AGAINST KONOHA'S OWN CANDIDATES.
WHY TEST US ALL TOGETHER?
MAINLY TO MAINTAIN THE SKILL OF ALL SHINOBI AT THE SAME HIGH LEVEL OF EXCELLENCE. ALSO TO FOSTER FRIENDSHIP AND UNDERSTANDING BETWEEN NINJA. AND, OF COURSE, TO MAINTAIN THE BALANCE OF POWER BETWEEN THE LANDS THEMSELVES.

POP
HEY! YOU THERE! WHAT'S YOUR NAME?
LISTEN, YOU! WHEN YOU ASK SOMEONE A QUESTION, IT'S CONSIDERED GOOD MANNERS TO LISTEN TO THEIR ENTIRE ANSWER.
HEY, KONOHAMARU! MAYBE I SHOULD ENTER THIS CHŪNIN SELECTION EXAM THING TOO, HUH?
FUMM
!
!
...
I WAS TALKING TO THE SPOOK BESIDE YOU.
NO!
W-WHO, ME?
HUH?
!
AND YOU ARE...?
...
GAARA OF THE DESERT, AT YOUR SERVICE.

UCHIHA SASUKE.
HEH
HEY! HEY! DON'T YOU WANT TO KNOW MY NAME?
NO.
LET'S GO.
...
TAK

SHHM
SHHM
SHHM
THINGS ARE GETTING INTERESTING.
KONOHAMARU, DO I LOOK LIKE SUCH A LOSER?
NEXT TO SASUKE, BIG GUY... YEAH.
SNIFF
SASUKE!! I AIN'T GONNA TAKE THIS!
WHERE DO YOU GET OFF STICKING YOUR NOSE IN?
WHAT DO YOU THINK?
NONE OF THEM ARE OF ANY IMPORTANCE...
...EXCEPT THE KONOHA RAVEN-HAIR AND THE SPOOK FROM THE SAND. KEEP AN EYE ON THEM.

KISHIMOTO MASASHI'S

POINTLESS LITTLE STORY

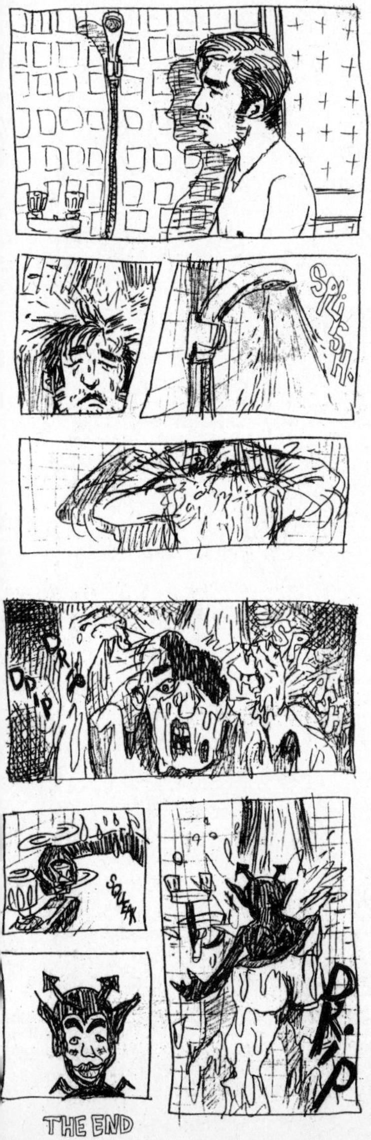

THE EIGHT-FRAME *MANGA* ON THE LEFT BRINGS BACK FOND MEMORIES FOR ME OF KOISHI, THE FRIEND WHO DREW IT FOR ME BACK IN COLLEGE. I HAD BEEN DRAWING *MANGA* SINCE MY HIGH-SCHOOL DAYS, BUT I DIDN'T HAVE A SINGLE FRIEND WHO SHARED MY PASSION. IN COLLEGE, I HEARD OF A GROUP OF MANGA FANS AND ASPIRING ARTISTS WHO CALLED THEMSELVES THE *MANKEN*, OR MANGA LAB. BUT THEY WEREN'T SO MUCH DRAWING MANGA AS THEY WERE PATTING EACH OTHER ON THE BACK FOR DRAWING PIN-UPS AND ILLUSTRATIONS WITH NO ATTEMPT AT STORYTELLING WHATSOEVER. I AVOIDED THOSE PHONIES LIKE THE PLAGUE AND WENT MY OWN WAY, TRYING TO DRAW ACTUAL MANGA.

THEN, ONE DAY, I MET A MAN WHO CLAIMED HE HAD DRAWN AUTHENTIC *MANGA* BACK IN HIGH SCHOOL. I HAD DOUBTS ABOUT WHETHER HE WAS ON THE LEVEL, SO I CHALLENGED HIM. I WAS DETERMINED TO FIND OUT WHETHER HE WAS A REAL MANGA ARTIST OR ANOTHER PHONY. I DEMANDED THAT HE DRAW A TWO-PAGE STORY FOR ME ON THE SPOT. SO HE DREW THE MANGA ON THE LEFT AND GAVE IT TO ME. IT WAS MOMENT OF INTENSE JOY FOR ME TO HOLD SOMEONE ELSE'S MANGA IN MY HAND LIKE THAT, FOR THE VERY FIRST TIME, AND I TREASURE HIS MANGA TO THIS VERY DAY.

36: SAKURA'S DEPRESSION

Number 36:
Sakura's Depression
IT ALL HAS A VERY SAD SOUND TO IT.

SLUMP
SHEESH!
SIGH
I MEAN, THINK HOW I FEEL. I OVERSLEPT, AND I DIDN'T EVEN GET TO BLOW-DRY MY HAIR!
SHE'S RIGHT! SAY IT, SAKURA!!
WE ⇨ CAN TELL
YEAH
WHY IS IT, WHENEVER WE GET CALLED OUT, WE END UP WAITING LIKE DOPES FOR THE CHALLENGER TO SHOW?
OKAY, LOOK! ARE WE GOING TO JUST STAND AROUND AND LET THEM GET AWAY WITH THIS?
WHY DO THESE TWO ALWAYS WAKE UP FEELING DRAMATIC?
EWWW! GROSS!
HEH...
RRRR
GRRR GRRR
YEAH. IT'S NOT RIGHT. I OVERSLEPT, TOO...
... AND I DIDN'T EVEN PAUSE TO WASH MY FACE OR BRUSH MY TEETH!

MORNING, GUYS!!
TODAY, I WANDERED A BIT FROM THE PATH OF LIFE...
!!
YOU ARE SUCH A LIAR!!
WOULD IT KILL YOU TO AT LEAST PRETEND TO BE SORRY?
IN ANY CASE...
THIS MAY SURPRISE YOU...
BUT I'VE RECOMMENDED ALL THREE OF YOU FOR THE *CHŪNIN* SELECTION EXAM.
HUH?!
...
!
SAY WHAT?!
GOOD ONE, MASTER. YOU ALMOST HAD US.
YOU HAVE TO FILL OUT APPLICATIONS.
JOURNEYMAN

MASTER KAKASHI, I LOVE YOU!!
GRAB
GET OFF... YOU'RE EMBARRASSING ME!
...
HEH HEH HEH HEH
IF ANY OF YOU DON'T WISH TO COMPETE, THE EXAM IS ENTIRELY VOLUNTARY.
THE CHOICE IS YOURS.
YOU NEEDN'T TURN IN THOSE APPLICATION FORMS UNLESS YOU WANT TO.
IF YOU DO, REPORT TO ROOM 301 AT THE SCHOOL BY 4:00 TOMORROW AFTERNOON.
THAT'S ALL!
FWMM

I'LL BET THERE'LL BE A LOT OF TOUGH COMPETITION.
TAK
DUM-DI-DI-DUH... THE JOURNEYMAN NINJA SELECTION EXAM!
TAK
I SWEAR, I AM NOT GONNA LET ANYONE BEAT ME!!
!
AND THAT OTHER ONE!!
RARRR
LIKE HIM!!
PLIT
YYYAYYY!
REPLACED BY NARUTO... I GUESS THE BEST MAN WON...
HEE HEE HEE!
TIME FOR THIS SENILE OLD FOOL TO RETIRE!
IF I COULD WIN SOMETHING THIS BIG... I
IN HIS DREAMS!
YA AY
PHOOEY
...IT'D BE SMOOTH SAILING TO BECOME THE NEXT LORD HOKAGE!
2

READ THIS WAY
...
I MIGHT GET TO FACE OFF AGAINST THAT SPOOK.
SHIVER
HAH!
...
LA-DI-DI-DA
...
...!
...DON'T WANT TO.
FORGET SASUKE... I CAN'T EVEN KEEP UP WITH NARUTO.
THIS EXAM WOULD BE TOO MUCH FOR ME.

THE NEXT DAY....
酒酒屋
HEY, SAKURA!
UH... HI.
...
WHAT'S... UP WITH HER?
IS THIS WHERE I SIGN MY NAME?
CAN'T YOU READ?
NINJA ACADEMY
忍
RUSH RUSH

IS SOMEONE AS TALENTLESS AS YOU REALLY PLANNING TO TAKE THE *CHŪNIN* SELECTION EXAM?
WHY BOTHER?
BUNCH OF WET-BEHIND-THE-EARS SNOTNOSES!
SNERK
YOU SAID IT!
PLEASE... WE'RE BEGGING YOU... LET US IN.
301
TAK
TAK
301
UHN-
!!
...THAT'S JUST CRUEL...!

WHAT DID YOU SAY?
YOU MISUNDER-STAND!
WE'RE JUST TRYING TO SPARE YOU...
THE *CHŪNIN* EXAM IS INCREDIBLY DIFFICULT... AND WE SHOULD KNOW. WE'VE FAILED THREE TIMES SO FAR.
THERE ARE PEOPLE WHO MADE IT, THEN IMMEDIATELY GAVE UP BEING SHINOBI... OTHERS WHO ENDED UP CRIPPLED... SOME REDUCED TO VEGETABLES... WE'VE SEEN IT ALL!
!!
WHOA
AW, MAN
BESIDES THAT, *CHŪNIN* ARE CELL COMMANDERS. THEY LEAD THEIR UNITS.
THE RESPONSIBILITIES FOR FAILED MISSIONS AND DEAD SHINOBI REST FIRMLY ON THEIR SHOULDERS.
AND YOU LITTLE PUNKS HAVE THE NERVE TO APPLY?
SNORT

THAT SOUNDS GOOD IN THEORY...
WE'RE SAVING A STEP BY WEEDING OUT THE OBVIOUS LOSERS BEFOREHAND.
301
WHAT'S HE TALKING ABOUT?
WHO KNOWS?
...!
I HAVE BUSINESS ON THE THIRD FLOOR.
TAK
... BUT YOU'D BETTER LET ME THROUGH.
AND DROP THE FORCE-FIELD ILLUSION YOU'VE CREATED, WHILE YOU'RE AT IT.
SO YOU FIGURED THAT OUT, EH?
301
HEH...

IT WAS EASY. RIGHT, SAKURA?
YOU WERE PROBABLY THE FIRST TO NOTICE IT.
HUH...?
YOU'RE THE MOST ANALYTICAL AND THE BEST IN OUR CELL...
...AT UNDERSTANDING THE ART OF ILLUSION.
WINK
...
SASUKE...
...
?
...THANK YOU!..
HEH.
OF COURSE I NOTICED IT.
OBVIOUSLY, WE'RE STILL ON THE SECOND FLOOR.

READ THIS WAY
OF COURSE!
30!
FWM
201
HEY... NOT BAD.
BUT JUST SEEING THROUGH IT ISN'T...
SNORT
...ENOUGH!!
SWOP
!!
WHAP WHAP
!!
SH HHM

HE'S SO FAST!!
HE PERCEIVED THE ATTACK PATTERNS ON BOTH SIDES AND PLANTED HIMSELF AT THE NEXUS OF BOTH THEIR KICKS... IS THAT EVEN POSSIBLE?!
HE'S A COMPLETELY DIFFERENT PERSON FROM THE BOY WHO WAS GETTING BEATEN UP JUST A MINUTE AGO.
SLUMP
FWWU
HE BLOCKED MY KICK!
BUT THERE'S SOMETHING WEIRD ABOUT HIS CHAKRA.
WHEW
HEY...

READ THIS WAY

WOULD YOU LIKE TO GO OUT WITH ME?
I'LL PROTECT YOU WITH MY LIFE!
GLEAM
NO...
...WAY.
YOU ARE WAY OUT OF HAND!
AWWW
HEE HEE!
HEY, YOU!
STEP
WHAT'S YOUR NAME?

READ THIS WAY

BONNG
HEH... SO THOSE ARE KAKASHI AND GUY'S PRECIOUS BRATS, EH? WELL, AT LEAST THEY MANAGED TO SUBMIT APPLICATIONS.
YEP.
NOW! SASUKE, NARUTO, LET'S GO!!
IT LOOKS LIKE WE CAN AMUSE OURSELVES WITH THIS YEAR'S CROP.
SNORT
A LITTLE PERK FOR BEING THE PROCTORS.
...
LET'S GO, LEE. WHAT ARE YOU DOING?
STOP PULLING.
TRA LA LA
SIGH

READ THIS WAY

TO BE CONTINUED IN **NARUTO** VOL.5!

IN THE NEXT VOLUME…

The Journeyman Ninja Selection Exams have begun… with a written test! Yes, brace yourself for a full volume of white-hot test-taking action! But all is not as it seems in the quiet exam hall. In a test of *ninjutsu*, it's not what you know that counts… it's what you can steal. To pass the exam, Naruto and his classmates will have to use every *shinobi* trick at their disposal to cheat! And they'd better cheat well, because if they can't answer the final question, they'll be barred from becoming ninja… *forever.*

AVAILABLE NOW!

SUBSCRIBE TODAY & BECOME A MEMBER OF THE SHONEN JUMP SUBSCRIBER CLUB...
You'll get:
*Access to Exclusive Online Content!
*50% Savings Off the Newsstand Price!
*Exclusive Premiums!
All this available ONLY to Subscribers!
SHONEN JUMP
THE WORLD'S MOST POPULAR MANGA ™
FILL OUT THE SUBSCRIPTION CARD ON THE OTHER SIDE, OR SUBSCRIBE ONLINE AT:
www.shonenjump.com